GET DRESSED!

A HISTORICAL GUESSING GAME FOR FASHION LOVERS

BY **KATY CANALES**

ILLUSTRATED BY **ERIN VANESSA**

For Matty, my constant inspiration
and to Rico for all the love, support
and cups of coffee. – KC

To JJ, my best-dressed, dear friend. – EV

Take a look inside the wardrobes of history's most fashionable people!

Over the years, humans have dressed in all kinds of clothing, from the perfectly practical to the potentially perilous.

They've fashioned fabulous frocks from feathers and fur, shimmied in stylish new silhouettes and catwalked in colourful clothing – or in some cases, nothing at all!

Journey to ten eras throughout history to find out what people wore. Each era showcases the way four different sets of people dressed in this time. Two of the clothing items for each set of people are accurate, and one is not!

Can you sort the fashion fact from fiction?

Were green eyebrows ever a fashion trend?

Did a queen really wear a giant ship in her wig?

And did people of the past avoid mud by using stilts?

  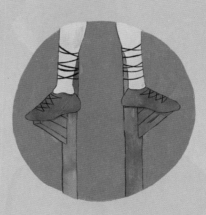

It's time to guess how people dressed!

What did people wear at the ANCIENT GREEK OLYMPICS?

Ancient Greece, 1000 BCE–1 CE

Around 3,000 years ago, the city states of ancient Greece were regularly at war with each other. Most Greeks lived in villages and worked on the land or fished in the surrounding sea, and many young men served in their nearby city's army. Despite the warfare, theatre, art and architecture flourished. Greeks believed in many gods and goddesses, who were said to watch over them from Mount Olympus. In 776 BCE the first recorded Olympic Games took place at Olympia in honour of Zeus, the king of the gods. The Games were held every four years for over 1,000 years and were the inspiration for today's Olympic Games. Under the watchful gaze of the Greek gods, what do you think athletes and spectators wore to the Ancient Olympic Games?

LONG ROBES

SUNGLASSES

COATS

TUNICS

STRAW HATS

FABRIC HEADBANDS

Children

Only wealthy boys were educated, starting school when they were seven years old. Their lessons included reading, writing and wrestling! Girls did not go to school but were taught at home how to cook, clean, look after children and weave their own cloth. What clothes might girls have made for themselves and their siblings?

Women

Women were only allowed to venture to a few places outside of their homes. It was illegal for married women to watch the Olympic Games, and those who did risked being thrown off Mount Typaion! If you were unmarried, you were allowed to watch the Olympic Games but the journey to Olympia could be a long one, so what do you think they would have worn?

SANDALS

HELMETS

OLIVE WREATHS

LEGGINGS

LOINCLOTHS

LONG TUNICS

Athletes

Being athletic was thought to be a sign of being a good person. Sport was so important that for the Olympic Games, truces were called between warring states and people travelled hundreds of kilometres, often on foot, to attend. Modern athletes wear stretchy sportswear, but what would the ancient Greeks have competed in?

Chariot riders

Four-horse chariot races were first introduced into the Olympic Games in 680 BCE. They were the first and most impressive competition of the games. The power, speed, cost and clamour of the chariot races made them compelling contests to watch and highly dangerous to take part in. This sport was open to women but only as chariot owners, not as racers.

At the ANCIENT GREEK OLYMPICS

children wore ...

TUNICS
Once boys turned seven years old, they wore short tunics to keep covered and cool.

AND

LONG ROBES
Girls wore long tunics called *peplos*, which were folded and then fastened at the shoulders and made of lightweight material.

BUT NOT ...

COATS
A wrap called a *himation* was worn over the shoulder and across the body. Structured items like coats had not been invented yet.

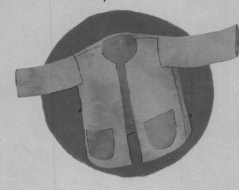

While very young children would have worn little to no clothes, older children dressed in clothing similar to adults. Girls' and boys' tunics were fastened at the waist with a belt to adjust their robe to the desired length. Worn over that, a *himation* would have provided protection from the summer sun.

women wore ...

FABRIC HEADBANDS
A simple headband fastened women's long hair in a bun. The style is the 'Knidian' after the stunning Knidian Aphrodite statue.

AND

STRAW HATS
Women wore straw hats with wide brims and a cloth head covering to protect them from the sun.

BUT NOT ...

SUNGLASSES
Sunglasses weren't invented until the 15th century in China.

Women were not allowed to compete at all in these Games but in later years unmarried women competed in the Heraean Games, which were held in honour of Hera, Queen of the gods and goddesses. At these games women competed wearing their hair loose, with shorter tunics that covered one shoulder, leaving the right shoulder and breast bare.

athletes wore ...

OLIVE WREATHS
No gold medals were awarded, but winners were crowned with ceremonial olive wreaths called *kotinos*.

AND

LOINCLOTHS
Men first competed wearing a *perizoma*, a type of loincloth held up by a band of fabric that went around the waist.

BUT NOT ...

SANDALS
Adults wore sandals if travelling far but athletes ran barefoot.

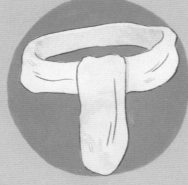

Athletes often competed wearing only a loincloth, with olive oil smeared on themselves to clean off dust and because they thought it made them look good. It is believed that in 720 BCE Orsippus became the first naked Olympic athlete when his perizoma dropped off during a race. From that point, athletes competed nude.

chariot riders wore ...

LONG TUNICS
Chariot riders wore long tunics, which were fixed with belts and shoulder straps to prevent them ballooning.

AND

LEGGINGS
To protect their legs, some chariot riders wore clothing similar to today's leggings.

BUT NOT ...

HELMETS
Unlike warriors, who wore metal helmets with brightly coloured mohawks, chariot riders wore only a headband to keep their hair down.

Despite being dragged behind four galloping horses on a small two-wheeled, open-backed wooden chariot, the riders had little in the way of protective clothing. They were equipped only with a whip to prompt the horses and a dagger to cut the reins if they lost control! In contrast, the horses were highly decorated with jewels woven into their manes and tails.

What did people wear in the **EARLY IRON AGE?**

Denmark, 500 BCE–400 CE

Denmark is now supposedly one of the happiest countries to live in, but 2,000 years ago the people living there had a tough life. Around this time period the climate changed, causing colder, wetter weather. People relied heavily on having warm summers with good harvests to ensure they had food to survive the bitterly cold winters. Many lived in small villages, kept livestock and ploughed the fields. Their clothes were made from the plants they grew or from the animals they kept. Most households wove their own clothes, sewing them together with sewing needles made from the bones from bird's feet. What clothes did people make for themselves in these hard times?

UMBRELLAS

POCKET KNIVES

EAR COVE

BEADED SKIRTS

TUNICS WITH POCKETS

WOOLLEN SHOES

Women

Women led short, hardworking lives in Iron Age Denmark. They looked after the livestock, ploughed and weeded the fields, harvested the crops, spun the wool, created the clothes, cared for children and made sure that there were two meals on the table every day for everyone to eat. What do you think they wore to stay warm and dry?

Children

Children played an important part in securing food for their families. In the summer and autumn children would have helped their relatives look after their flocks of sheep as well as forage and dry a range of foods like mushrooms, fruits and nuts. What do you think Early Iron Age children wore?

STILTS

TASSELLED
BELTS

LEG
WRAPPINGS

ANIMAL-HIDE SHOES

TROUSERS

WOOLLEN
CAPES

Peat cutters

Peat coal was used at this time as it burned better than wood, so peat cutters harvested it in blocks from bogs. Bogs were considered sacred places, where sacrifices and offerings were made. The demand for weapons and iron goods meant that more fuel was needed to keep the fires burning to smelt the iron. How did peat cutters dress for this muddy work?

Blacksmiths

The Iron Age began when Danes started extracting and using local iron, rather than importing expensive bronze. Iron was more versatile so blacksmiths could make a wider range of products. As battles between neighbouring countries broke out, iron weapons were vital for keeping the enemy at bay. What would blacksmiths have worn to work?

In the EARLY IRON AGE

women wore ...

WOOLLEN SHOES
Wool wasn't just used for their mittens! On their feet they wore woollen shoes.

AND

BEADED SKIRTS
Their corded skirts were embellished with beads made from animal teeth and metal, which tinkled when they moved.

BUT NOT ...

UMBRELLAS
Umbrellas were used in Egypt and China but in Denmark, women sheltered from the rain under felted wool cloaks or animal pelts.

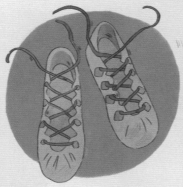  

Living by a peat bog may not sound glamorous but Danish women did have an eye for fashion. They wore brightly coloured blouses embroidered with different yarns and intricate patterns. Their clothing was decorated with elaborate oval-shaped discs and beaded necklaces. Hair was worn long and styled in very elaborate braids.

children wore ...

EAR COVERS
In the chilly winters children kept their ears warm with woollen headscarves or sheepskin hats with ear flaps.

AND

POCKET KNIVES
Children carried knives to be used as tools and for protection.

BUT NOT ...

TUNICS WITH POCKETS
There were no pockets in their clothing. Instead, purses were worn on their belt to keep their coins in.

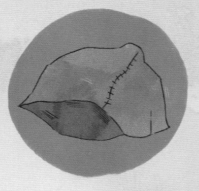  

Girls wore a long-sleeved dress fastened at the waist with a drawstring. On top was a sleeveless dress made from colourful chequered patterned cloth and fasten by large brooches. Young boys wore drawstring trousers and over that a woollen tunic that hung down to their knees. Boys had a cloak that fastened on one shoulder.

peat cutters wore ...

TASSELLED BELTS
The leather belt worn by peat cutters would have had complex tassels. Iron embellishments were reserved for the powerful.

 AND

LEG WRAPPINGS
Strips of cloth called puttees wrapped around their trousers prevented water and mud seeping into their shoes and up their legs.

 BUT NOT ...

STILTS
The bogs were very deep so stilts would not have been much use as they would have sunk into the ground.

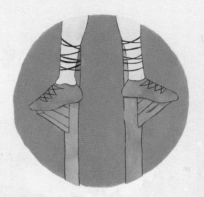

Cutting peat and transporting it back from the peat bogs was hard manual work. Men's clothes needed to be as tough as their owners. To protect them from the extreme weather, they wore cloaks, hats and wound strips of cloth around their shins to keep their legs and shoes dry. They wore trousers and a tunic with a leather belt fastened over it.

blacksmiths wore ...

TROUSERS
Trousers kept their legs warm and protected. The Greeks and Romans considered trousers to be crude and the clothing of barbarians.

AND

ANIMAL-HIDE SHOES
Blacksmiths wore shoes made of animal hide that wrapped around the feet to keep them warm and dry.

 BUT NOT ...

WOOLLEN CAPES
Blacksmiths would have worn surprisingly little as the forge was so hot, so just a sleeveless tunic and trousers. No capes needed inside!

Working with molten iron in a forge would have been hot, dangerous work. Two thousand years ago, there was not much protective clothing available and blacksmiths would have relied on a leather apron to shield them from the sparks. Outside of the forge, wealthy blacksmiths could have had decoratively woven edges on their trousers and tops.

What did people wear in the TANG DYNASTY?

China, 618–907 CE

The Tang dynasty in China was one of the greatest empires in the world. It is the only time in China's history that a woman has been its ruler. Its imperial court in Chang'an (present-day Xi'an) was the most populated city in the world. In Chang'an you could find everything from live rhinos to glittering rubies. Made rich from trade, the Tang imperial court was a focus for music, poetry and fashion. The variety of textiles available included wool, leopard skin and gold thread. What do you think people wore during this dynasty?

HAIR BUNS

HELMETS

BELTED TUNICS

MOHAIR COATS

BAGGY TROUSERS

POINTED SLIPPERS

Musicians

The imperial court welcomed visitors from around the world. Playing music helped to keep the mood lively and everyone entertained. The key instruments played at this time were the bamboo pipes, flute and stringed instruments such as the zither and the lute. What do you think musicians wore when performing for important guests?

Female polo players

Horse-riding was a popular activity for both men and women from noble families. The Persian game of polo, in which two teams ride on horses and use a mallet to try to hit a small ball into a goal, was a great favourite. Women during the Tang dynasty did not ride sidesaddle but had both feet in the stirrups to have greater control! What do you think they wore to play?

GOLD MEDALLIONS

HAIR ACCESSORIES

PAINTED EYEBROWS

OFFICIAL MILITARY DRESS

HATS

MONOCHROME ROBES

Poets

Poets were educated members of the court and their writings recorded big events, ideas and the natural world. Poets in Tang China invented new styles of poetry. Some poets were known to hide complaints behind their beautiful words, but it was a brave poet who criticized Empress Wu. What would they wear to entertain the imperial court?

Empress Wu

Wu Zetian was not born into the Tang imperial family, but rose in rank by removing rivals to become the Tang emperor's consort. When this emperor died, Wu Zetian stepped in and ruled China for 40 years. During this time Empress Wu made laws to stop certain materials leaving the country. What would she wear to show her status and power?

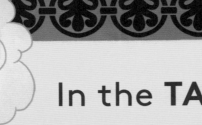

In the **TANG DYNASTY**

musicians wore ...

HAIR BUNS
Tang women wore their hair in singular or double topknots. These were decorated with ornaments.

AND

POINTED SLIPPERS
They wore slippers with curved, pointed tips that poked out from the bottom of their long skirts, protecting the wearer from tripping up.

BUT NOT ...

MOHAIR COATS
Instead of coats, musicians wrapped a long, thin shawl called a *pibo* around their body to keep warm.

At the Tang court, celebrated groups of female musicians would perform while seated on the floor. They wore a low-cut robe called a *shan* under a short-sleeved jacket called a *banbi*, which was tucked under a high-waisted striped skirt and secured by a patterned belt. Their slippers were made of a range of materials, with silk damask being used for the finest shoes.

female polo players wore ...

BELTED TUNICS
Influenced by styles from neighbouring countries, women wore *hufu*, a belted knee-length tunic with splits up the sides.

AND

BAGGY TROUSERS
Underneath their tunic, they wore loose trousers that gathered at the ankle and tucked into high, soft boots.

BUT NOT ...

HELMETS
Instead of helmets, they wore a *weimao*, a curtain hat with a gauzed veil that was pulled back to show the face.

Many Tang women were excellent horse riders. They adopted foreign styles and wore light, loose clothes including tunics with turned-down-collars and baggy trousers or breeches so they could ride centre saddle. Whether in court or on horseback, noble women wore luxurious materials and ornate hairstyles.

poets wore ...

MONOCHROME ROBES
Strict laws controlled who could wear certain fabrics and colours, so poets wore long loose robes in simple colours such as white or black.

AND

HATS
Poets would not have ventured out without their *futou*, a black hat made of cloth with wings that fell downwards.

BUT NOT ...

GOLD MEDALLIONS
Poets did not wear flashy, expensive accessories. They preferred simple outfits.

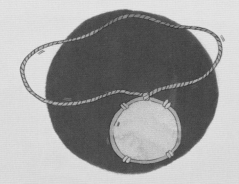

Poets modelled themselves after the celebrated Chinese philosopher Confucius, adopting simple, sombre clothing and rejecting luxuries. They treated sacrificial and ceremonial clothing with the highest respect. Poets like Wang Jian and Bai Juyi wrote about the hard work of the silk weavers and criticized fashion followers for spending their money on silks.

Empress Wu wore ...

PAINTED EYEBROWS
Eyebrows were shaved off and green stubby patches resembling a silkworm moth – an insect associated with riches – were painted on top.

AND

HAIR ACCESSORIES
Empress Wu wore hair pins, jewelled accessories and false hair buns, The bigger the hair, the more important the wearer.

BUT NOT ...

OFFICIAL MILITARY DRESS
Empress Wu would have worn patterned silk robes. Her daughter, Taiping Princess, did wear official military dress for an imperial banquet, though!

Materials such as yaks' tails and patterned damask silks were not to leave the country, and some materials were forbidden for the lower classes to wear. Empress Wu and female court members wore gowns embroidered with shapes, animals or flowers. Empress Wu sometimes wore an electric-blue headdress made with kingfisher feathers.

What did people wear in the **OTTOMAN EMPIRE?**

Middle East, Eastern Europe & North Africa, 1299–1922

The Ottoman Empire was founded in what is now Turkey by Sultan Osman I (1258–1326). Over the next 600 years, the empire expanded to cover 43 present-day countries including Romania, Yemen and Egypt. The empire brought together a wealth of textiles and techniques from silk and metal threads to woven and embroidered fabrics. By the 1700s textile manufacturing had reached its peak as stunning designs, skilled workers and beautiful materials met to make new outfits for the whole court to take part in the sultans' opulent ceremonies.

ANIMAL EMBROIDERY

GOLD CHAINS

GOLDEN ROBES

KAFTANS

FUR-LINED ROBES

SANDALS

The sultan

Sultans were the leaders of the Ottoman Empire and wielded immense political, military and religious control. It was common for sultans to give reams of valuable silk, or 'robes of honour' called *hil'at* to important people to mark special occasions and build alliances. What do you think sultans wore to demonstrate their power and privilege?

Venetian ambassadors

Silk played a huge part in the Empire's trading success, making it wealthy and powerful. As Italy was the epicentre of the world's finest silk and velvet-making industries, Ottoman and Italian ambassadors helped strike trade deals to ensure that the Italians continued to supply sumptuous materials fit for a sultan. What do you think Venetian ambassadors wore while travelling?

HEADDRESSES

RED VELVET ROBES

ELASTICATED BRACES

SOFT SLIPPERS

TROUSERS

WOODEN CLOGS

Skilled masters

At its peak in 1600, the palace employed 600–900 master craftspeople, who worked in the imperial workshops. Artists were gathered from defeated cities across the empire or invited from Europe to come live in the palace, train new artists and create books, jewellery, tiles, textiles and more. How did artists express their creativity through clothes?

Female embroiderers

Women played an active but secretive role in the Ottoman Empire's textile production. They were outlawed from many of the craftspeople's guilds and the imperial workshops, but they could work from home and produce fine pieces of embroidery by hand, which they sold to merchants. What do you think women wore?

In the **OTTOMAN EMPIRE**

sultans wore ...

KAFTANS
The sultan wore layers of long robes, called kaftans, which protected him from the cold and made him look bigger and more imposing.

AND

FUR-LINED ROBES
On top of the kaftan the sultan would wear a long outer robe with fur lining, often from ermines or sables.

BUT NOT ...

ANIMAL EMBROIDERY
Due to Islamic beliefs no figures of animals or people were allowed to be featured on the fabric used for the sultan's clothing.

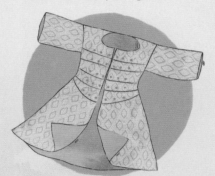 

The kaftans were made of luxurious woven silk fabrics decorated in detailed geometric patterns that held symbolic meanings. From 1600 many sultans wore lucky shirts embroidered with words and numbers that referred to verses from the holy book, the Qur'an, as well as secret codes.

Venetian ambassadors wore ...

GOLD CHAINS
These were often given by Sultans as thanks for their service. The quality of a gift from a Sultan reflected how important you were to them.

AND

GOLDEN ROBES
Robes made of a gold cloth, called *seraser* were the most prized gifts for ambassadors to receive from the sultan.

BUT NOT ...

SANDALS
Venetian ambassadors would have worn leather shoes, not sandals.

Official ambassadors wore a red toga with a stole draped over their shoulder, and a black cap. The robe's vivid scarlet or crimson colour, as well as its sumptuous materials like velvet and silk damask, reflected the ambassador's status and the importance of their role. It also set them apart from the rest of the ambassadorial group, who wore black.

skilled masters wore ...

SOFT SLIPPERS
These slip-on shoes were made of soft leather and embellished with geometric designs in colourful or golden threads.

AND

HEADDRESSES
A cap called a *sarık* was wrapped with a shroud called a *kavuk*. The style, colour and material reflected the wearer's power.

BUT NOT ...

RED VELVET ROBES
The colour red and the fabric velvet were reserved for the nobility.

Skilled master craftspeople would have enjoyed high status in the palace and this would have been reflected in their clothes. A skilled artist would have worn a *kavuk* headdress and a jacket called a *cübbe* or *hırka* over a long kaftan. Under that he would wear baggy trousers called *salvar*.

female embroiderers wore ...

TROUSERS
Women wore baggy salvar trousers, which gathered tightly at the ankles.

AND

WOODEN CLOGS
On their feet women would have worn raised wooden clogs, or *nalın*.

BUT NOT ...

ELASTICATED BRACES
These were only introduced about 200 years ago. Ottoman women's trousers were held up by drawstrings, sashes or belts.

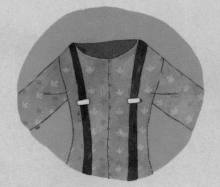

Women's clothing often had slightly smaller-scale patterns but other than that they wore similar clothes to men. Both wore clothing that was loose and covered their bodies from head to toe. Over a light undershirt and trousers, women wore a long robe called an *entari*. If leaving the house, they would wear a face or head covering called a *yashmak* or *niqab*.

What did people wear in the
INCA STATE?

Inca state, 1438–1532

At its height, the Inca Empire ruled over 10 million people and spanned 3,000 miles from the Pacific Ocean to the Amazon and across the Andes mountains. The Incas were incredible engineers and built extensive networks of roads, waterways, suspension bridges and structures that survived countless earthquakes. They developed complex farming and communication methods over the tough terrain. Despite its vast size the Inca Empire was run by an efficient government called the *Tawantinsuyu*, which controlled all aspects of Inca life, including what people could wear.

EMBROIDERED BELTS

CLOTHES PINS

HAND-WOVEN BAGS

WELLINGTON BOOTS

DECORATIVE DRESSES

CLOAKS

Herders

South America is home to millions of llamas and alpacas. These fluffy four-legged creatures can live on mountains in freezing conditions. They were prized by the Incas as they provided transport, meat and wool. Herders led their animals through the steep mountainsides in search of new pastures to graze. How did they dress when working?

Weavers

Clothing reflected the wearer's wealth and status. Events, as well as state and regional symbols, were woven into the cloth. All households wove cloth, but highly skilled weavers, called *acllacuna*, were employed by the state to supply clothing for the nobility. What do you think they wove to wear themselves?

FEATHERED HEADDRESSES

MILITARY EPAULETTES

KNOTTED THREADS

A CROWN

GEOMETRIC PATTERNS

FLUFFY SLIPPERS

The Sapa Inca

The Sapa Inca was the supreme leader and head of the *Tawantinsuyu*, the military and the religion. Believed to be a descendant of the sun god, Inti, he was worshipped by all. He was so powerful that eye contact was not allowed, and he was carried by his servants everywhere he went on a golden platform called a litter. What would he have worn?

The Coya Inca

The Coya was the sister and first wife of the Sapa Inca, as the Inca could have many wives. The Coya was considered the 'queen of all women' and led the worshipping of Killa, the moon goddess. The Coya was the second-in-command after the Sapa Inca and wielded sizeable political and religious power. What did this powerful woman choose to wear?

In the INCA STATE

herders wore ...

EMBROIDERED BELTS
Herders wore a belt around their tunic. The belts were elaborately hand-woven with symbolic details.

AND

HAND-WOVEN BAGS
Beautiful hand-woven double-sided tapestries were made into bags for the herders to carry their provisions in.

BUT NOT ...

WELLINGTON BOOTS
Wellies were only invented about 200 years ago. Incas wore leather sandals in the summer and wool-lined slippers in the winter.

Over a loincloth, herders would wear a simple tunic called an *unqo*. It was made from a single sheet folded in half and sewn together at the sides with openings for the arms and neck. To keep them warm and dry as they scrambled after their herd, herders would wear a cloak or a poncho made from llama and alpaca wool.

weavers wore ...

CLOAKS
A cloak known as a *lliclla*, pinned at the front, kept its wearer warm, dry and protected from the sun.

AND

CLOTHES PINS
Ornamental clothes pins, called *tupu*, doubled as knives.

BUT NOT ...

DECORATIVE DRESSES
The *acllacuna* were able to make all kinds of spectacular clothing, but they were not allowed to wear what they made as they were not noble.

 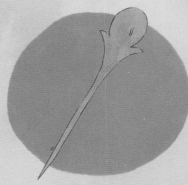 

Talented weavers from across Inca society could create complex double-sided designs with unlimited colour and pattern changes, but they were only allowed to wear simple clothing. They wore a long cloth that wrapped around their body. It was pinned at the shoulder and tied at the waist with a sash called a *chumpi*.

the Sapa Inca wore ...

FEATHERED HEADDRESS
The Sapa Inca wore a headdress made of a woollen fringe decorated with gold and feathers of a rare coraquenque bird.

AND

KNOTTED THREADS
Before the written word, ancient Incas communicated through a complex system of knotted coloured threads made from llama wool.

BUT NOT ...

MILITARY EPAULETTES
But his clothing did have shoulder pads and he is likely to have worn shin armour called greaves.

 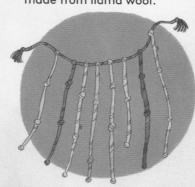 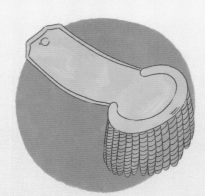

The Sapa Inca had clothing fit for a god. His clothes were covered with beautiful designs and precious jewels. Each day the Sapa Inca would put on new clothes and at the end of each day his clothes would be taken off and burnt. This meant that he went through a lot of clothes, and it ensured that skilled weavers were constantly busy.

the Coya Inca wore ...

GEOMETRIC PATTERNS
The complex geometric patterns on her shawl were called *T'oqapu*. Only the nobility were allowed to wear this pattern.

AND

FLUFFY SLIPPERS
In winter she wore slippers made of soft vicuña wool to keep her toes toasty!

BUT NOT ...

A CROWN
The Coya didn't wear a crown, but she did wear a headdress of woven cloth.

 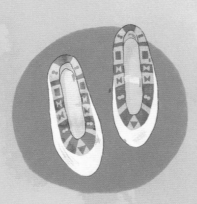 

The Coya's clothes reflected her powerful status. She was bedecked with jewels and gold. She wore intricately woven tapestry dresses that wrapped around her body. These dresses were belted with a beautifully embroidered *chumpi* sash. Draped over her shoulders she would have worn a rectangular *liclla* shawl.

What did people wear in the ELIZABETHAN ERA?

London, 1558–1603

Queen Elizabeth I (1533-1603) ruled over England and Ireland for 45 years. During her reign there was an explosion of inventions including flushing toilets, the telescope and the pencil. Uncharted parts of the world and the solar system were discovered and explored. It was a 'Golden Age' for art, music and theatre with the queen inspiring many of William Shakespeare's plays. Despite this, over half the population were living in poverty, and the gap between the poorest and richest was vast. Can you guess how people's clothes depended on their status?

UNDERWEAR

MONMOUTH CAPS

TUNICS

WOOL AND LINEN

PADDED JACKETS

GIRDLES

Farrier's apprentice

Orphaned children were sent to learn a trade and serve as an apprentice. It was important that they found work, as begging was punishable by death. Being a farrier's apprentice was a prized position. A farrier cared for horses' hooves and occasionally performed surgeries on animals and even people! What did apprentices wear to work?

Yeomen's daughters

A yeoman owned or rented land and paid people to work for him. His daughter would not have received an education but, unlike working-class girls, she would not have been sent out to work as a maid or a cook for other households. Instead she would have worked within the home or made items to sell. What do you think she would have worn?

DETACHABLE
SLEEVES

WRISTWATCHES

CARTWHEEL
RUFFS

PURPLE AND
GOLD

PADDED
STOCKINGS

POINTY
SHOES

Earls

Queen Elizabeth promoted very few people to positions of nobility as she knew that powerful lords had the money and the influence to challenge a monarch's authority. At court she kept her noblemen on their toes, bestowing favours to those who flattered her and ruining those who disobeyed. What would an earl have worn at court?

Queen Elizabeth

Elizabeth was the last of King Henry VIII's three children to be crowned. Despite not being first choice, she proved to be a popular and formidable leader. During her reign she successfully deflected plots to kill her, fought the Spanish Armada and resisted pressure from parliament to marry. What do you think she wore to show her power and wealth?

In the **ELIZABETHAN ERA**

a farrier's apprentice wore ...

MONMOUTH CAPS
According to law, men and boys above six years old had to wear a wool-knit cap on Sundays and holidays or pay a fine.

AND

TUNICS
Many working-class men wore a tunic as they were flexible and more affordable than breeches and a doublet (early shorts and jackets).

BUT NOT ...

UNDERWEAR
Men wore a codpiece, a removable padded piece of cloth that covered and protected the groin.

 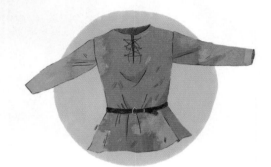 

A farrier's apprentice needed clothes that were sturdy and loose as he worked in dirty conditions doing hard physical work for little money. There were many tools of the trade that a farrier needed, but a leather apron was the hallmark of a skilled craftsperson. An apron would have been expensive and was passed down from a master to his apprentice.

yeomen's daughters wore ...

WOOL AND LINEN
Yeomen and their families were forbidden from wearing gold, silver, jewels, silk, embroidery or expensive furs so they wore wool and linen.

AND

GIRDLES
Men and women wore a girdle, a decorative belt from which they hung items like fans, purses or daggers.

BUT NOT ...

PADDED JACKETS
No, it was men who wore jackets called doublets. Doublets were padded to make them look bigger.

By law a yeoman's daughter would have worn modest, simple clothing but she could have added tiny flashes of a decorative trim to her clothes. Over a thin white linen dress called a chemise, she would have worn a woollen dress and an apron. On her head, she'd wear a simple linen cap called a coif and, below, knee-high stockings tied with ribbons and leather shoes.

earls wore ...

PADDED STOCKINGS
Men wore short breeches with knee-length stockings. Some men padded their silk stockings to make their calves look shapely!

AND

CARTWHEEL RUFFS
Men wore 20-centimetre-wide frilly collars called ruffs made from 5½ metres of lace, starched and folded into around 600 pleats.

BUT NOT ...

PURPLE AND GOLD
The wealthy wore layers of colourful fabrics decorated with lace, fur and jewels but only royalty wore gold or purple cloth, and ermine fur.

Powerful nobles could afford to follow the latest fashion trends from France and Italy, but there was a catch – everything had to be made in Britain due to strict import laws. Noblemen were spending so much money on clothing trying to impress Queen Elizabeth that she brought in laws to try to curb their shopping habits!

Queen Elizabeth I wore ...

WRISTWATCHES
In 1571 Queen Elizabeth was given a watch face enclosed in a jewelled bracelet by the Earl of Leicester. It is believed to be the first wristwatch.

AND

DETACHABLE SLEEVES
Women's outfits were made or up of 18 items fastened with pins and ties. Detachable items made varying an outfit more affordable.

BUT NOT ...

POINTY SHOES
By the Elizabethan era, pointy shoes were out of fashion and square-toed leather slip-on heeled shoes were popular.

Queen Elizabeth set many fashion trends. Her impressive dresses were made from opulent materials and were ladened with jewels and gold threads. Despite being queen, she was still expected to wear a tight corset to cinch her waist in, a padded tube called a 'bum-roll' and a hooped skirt called a 'farthingale' to push out her skirts.

What did people wear in the EDO ERA?

Japan, 1615–1868

Edo is the historical name of modern-day Tokyo and also an era in Japan. It was a time of peace, wealth and stability in Japan that saw Edo, the small fishing village, transform into one of the world's largest cities. Edo was the centre of politics and culture. People came to explore its entertainment districts packed with theatres, restaurants and clothing shops. Japan's rulers imposed restrictions on outside travel and trade but riches from across the world were still able to enter through controlled ports. Strict clothing laws were in place but people had clever ways of getting round them. Can you guess what Edo people were allowed to wear?

METAL MASKS

IRON-PLATED ARMOUR

LACED-UP KIMONOS

PAINTED BLACK TEETH

PLATFORM SANDALS

FLIP-FLOPS

Samurai

Samurai were trained warriors who were famed for their bravery and fighting skills. They came from noble families and served the local lords. Samurai were permitted to carry swords; a long one called a *katana* and a short one called a *tanto*. It was believed the swords held the samurai's soul. Can you guess what these highly respected fighters wore?

Geishas

Geishas were celebrated entertainers and storytellers. They started their training when they were young girls, living away from their families in geisha houses called *okiya*. There they learnt how to perform traditional Japanese arts, including singing, poetry and dancing. How do you think geishas dressed to welcome visitors to teahouses and social events?

DRAMATIC MAKE-UP

SYMBOLIC FABRIC

BLACK KIMONOS

REVERSIBLE JACKETS

BRACES

BODY TATTOOS

Kabuki actors

Kabuki is a centuries-old form of theatre combining music, dance, singing and extravagant costumes. Initially all the parts were played by women but during the Edo period that changed so only men were actors. Kabuki actors were highly celebrated in print, artworks and clothing. What do you think these superstars of the time wore when performing?

Firefighters

Edo was a city made of millions of wooden buildings. Frequent earthquakes meant that fires could break out and spread rapidly. Volunteer fire brigades were stationed in towers across the city to look out for fires and pull down burning buildings to stop fires spreading. What do you think firefighters wore for protection while doing this dangerous job?

In the **EDO ERA**

samurai wore ...

METAL MASKS
Some samurai wore full or half-length metal face masks complete with whiskers and moustaches.

AND

FLIP-FLOPS
In summer samurai wore a lightweight and comfortable form of flip-flops, called *waraji*, made of straw.

BUT NOT ...

IRON-PLATED ARMOUR
As this was a time of peace, the samurai switched from heavy iron-plated pieces to lighter leather pieces that were more comfortable.

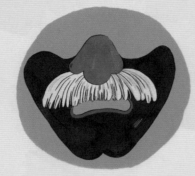  

The leather plates of a samurai's armour were held together by beautifully braided silk, which allowed the plates to move with the wearer. Along with the protective pieces for the arms, legs and shoulders, samurai wore a spectacular wide-brimmed helmet with a protective neck guard. A samurai's top-knot hairstyle made their helmets more comfortable to wear.

geishas wore ...

PLATFORM SANDALS
Geishas wore highly stylized, fashionable clothing. To keep it clean they wore platformed sandals called *geta*.

AND

PAINTED BLACK TEETH
Geishas painted their teeth black, believing it looked like luxurious black lacquer. This beauty feature was called *Ohaguro*.

BUT NOT ...

LACED-UP KIMONOS
Geishas wore handmade silk kimonos but they weren't laced – they were closed by a wide sash knotted at the back, called an *obi*.

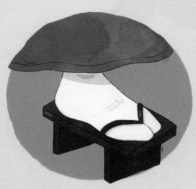  

The T-shaped kimono was worn by everyone. Kimonos could be simple, lightweight printed cotton robes but a geisha's kimonos were highly decorative. From their *obi* sash they hung a beautifully designed lacquered case called an *inro*, which held their personal items. These cases served as pockets since kimonos do not have any.

kabuki actors wore ...

SYMBOLIC FABRIC
Outfits often featured patterns that symbolized who the character was or was of the actor's or company's own crest.

AND

DRAMATIC MAKE-UP
Actors wore dramatic thick white, red, black and blue make-up so audiences could tell the goodies from the baddies.

BUT NOT ...

BLACK KIMONOS
Actors' robes were made to be dramatic so they were colourful, with padding, embellishment and elaborate bold designs.

Kabuki actors were easy to spot – they were extravagantly dressed and highly made-up with sections of their heads shaved. Their costumes varied depending on the role and each outfit held symbols and hints about the character. They wore several different layers, which they would shed throughout the performance.

firefighters wore ...

REVERSIBLE JACKETS
After extinguishing a fire, a firefighter would celebrate by reversing his jacket to show decorative characters from heroic myths.

AND

BODY TATTOOS
Edo firefighters were often covered with fire-themed tattoos. It was believed that the tattoos would protect them.

BUT NOT ...

BRACES
Modern-day firefighters wear braces to keep their trousers up but Edo firefighters would have worn an *obi* cloth sash.

Edo firefighters were real-life action heroes and were celebrated in print and kabuki plays. Many worked as steeplejacks building houses during the day and volunteered as firefighters at night. To protect themselves from flames, firefighters wore heavy quilted jackets soaked in water to prevent them from catching fire as well as thick cotton hats, trousers and gloves.

What did people wear in the
FRENCH REVOLUTION?
France, 1789–1799

King Louis XVI was not a good ruler. He wasted France's money on war and expensive things, including fancy clothing. During his reign, France had bad harvests and high taxes. The royal family's excessive spending made the public angry. On 14 July 1789 the people revolted, storming the state prison known as the Bastille, and went to war against the monarchy. Over the next ten years, many people died. The monarchy was overthrown, and in its place was a new system where the people voted for their leaders. The Republic of France began with the hope of making France a fairer place to live. The French Revolution changed fashion forever. What do you think people wore to show who they supported?

LOOSE DRESSES

TWO-PIECE SUITS

METAL ARMOUR

SOFT CAPS

STRIPY DRESSES

WOODEN CLOGS

Children

Many poor children fought in the French Revolution. They joined gangs and armed themselves with weapons. In wealthier households loyal to the king, children were often shielded from the battles but risked being caught by a mob or thrown into prison! During this time children's clothing also had a revolution.

Female revolutionaries

The revolution shook up France politically, socially and culturally. From seamstresses to servants, working women were active protestors. They took part in uprisings, and even marched to the Palace of Versailles to demand bread from the king. What styles do you think they wore when fighting for freedom?

EXTRAVAGANT WIGS

DRESSES WITH POCKETS

SILK SHOES

SHORT JACKETS

RED AND BLUE

RED-HEELED SHOES

Male revolutionaries

During the French Revolution clothing expressed which side people supported. Clothing could be political and sometimes deadly, as the style, colour and cut of the garments told others which of the warring sides you were on. What do you think men wore to show their support for the revolution?

Marie Antoinette

Marie Antoinette was the last queen of France. She loved fashion and reportedly never wore anything twice, buying over 300 gowns a year. Her style set fashion trends across Europe. What she wore was so important that she had a 'Minister of Fashion' to help dress and style her. Even after she was put in prison, Marie Antoinette was still having new clothes delivered.

In the FRENCH REVOLUTION

children wore ...

LOOSE DRESSES
Girls wore loose, high-waisted dresses that allowed them to sit, bend and run more freely than the corsets and hooped skirts they wore previously.

AND

TWO-PIECE SUITS
Boys sported two-piece suits, buttoned together at the waist. Although tight, they allowed boys more freedom than doublets and breeches.

BUT NOT ...

METAL ARMOUR
Armour protected from lances, swords and maces but not gunpower. It would have been too expensive for most people.

Children's clothes were no longer mini adult outfits and became more comfortable. Little babies were freed from dangerously tight swaddling that had once been popular, helping them to move their limbs and cool down as well as poo and wee. This reflected a big change in how children were valued and the growing interest in improving children's welfare.

female revolutionaries wore ...

STRIPY DRESSES
Many women keen to show their support for the Republic wore striped or patterned dresses in the colours of the French flag.

AND

WOODEN CLOGS
Often working women were barefoot. Those who could afford shoes had limited options. Wooden clogs, called *sabots*, were cheap.

BUT NOT ...

SOFT CAPS
Only men wore the *phrygian* cap. The headsquare bonnet worn instead by working women became a symbol of the revolutionaries.

Female revolutionaries showed their loyalty by wearing red-white-and-blue-coloured ribboned badges known as *cockades*. Unlike those who supported the monarchy, their clothes were simple and were usually made from affordable materials such as wool and cotton. After the French Revolution their simple clothing style became fashionable for all.

male revolutionaries wore ...

RED AND BLUE
Men wore red and blue clothing to reflect the ancient colours of Paris. Royal white was added later. The colours became the new French flag.

AND

SHORT JACKETS
They wore jackets known as *carmagnoles* that were less fancy than the long frock coats worn by the wealthy and powerful.

BUT NOT ...

RED-HEELED SHOES
Only nobles with access to the court were permitted to wear red-heeled shoes.

Revolutionaries wore simple clothes. The working-class people who took part in the French Revolution were nicknamed after the long trousers that working men wore – the *sans-culottes*. These trousers were shockingly different from the knee-length silk breeches worn by the wealthy elite and represented a revolution in clothing.

Marie Antoinette wore ...

EXTRAVAGANT WIGS
Marie Antoinette once went to a party wearing a wig that made her hair look like a stormy sea – it even had a ship in it.

AND

SILK SHOES
The queen had many heeled shoes that were made of expensive silk, kid leather and decorated with ribbons.

BUT NOT ...

DRESSES WITH POCKETS
Women's pockets were detachable and fastened around the waist with ties. Worn under clothes, they were the safest place for women to keep precious items.

Marie Antoinette's clothing brought her fame, but it also played a big part in her end. When her hair thinned, she started wearing horsehair wigs powdered with dry clay and white flour. Using flour for wigs caused outcry as people were struggling to buy flour for bread.

What did people wear in the ROARING TWENTIES?

United States of America, 1920–1929

In 1920s America, life moved fast. Manufacturing, technology and science industries were striving to create inventions that were bigger, faster, better and made more money! It was an age that saw cars rolling off the assembly lines and on to streets, electricity lighting up homes across the country, and some women finally winning the right to vote. Fashion also changed as new materials made luxury items cheaper to make and buy, and modern values saw young women and men throwing away the heavy fashions of the previous century. Can you guess what people wore in this exciting era? Which items do you think they didn't wear?

PETER PAN COLLARS

ZIP-UP CLOTHES

LONG TROUSERS

FLAT CAPS

HOUSE APRONS

HOOPED SKIRT

Children

When not attending school, many children worked. They sold newspapers, shined shoes or worked in factories or on farms. When they weren't working, radio and cinema offered exciting new forms of entertainment for them to enjoy. What do you think a child might have worn?

Factory workers

The growth in new manufacturing processes and products created new jobs. Men and women moved from the countryside to the towns to take up work in the car, radio and clothing factories. Can you guess what clothes they wore to protect themselves from sparks, dust and grease?

936

LONG, FLOWING HAIR

COLLAR PINS

KEYBOARD NECKTIES

BARE ARMS AND LEGS

SHORT, LOOSE DRESSES

FLASHY FOOTWEAR

Flappers

Flappers were free-spirited young American women. They loved parties and enjoyed more independence than ever before. They rebelled with their clothing choices, ditching the tight corsets and heavy clothing that their mothers wore. Can you guess what shocking clothing they might have picked to party in?

Jazz musicians

Across America's cities, nightclubs thrummed with jazz, a modern, dynamic sound that was a stark contrast to the music before it. In a divided America, music by artists of colour like Louis Armstrong and Duke Ellington cut across race and class, appealing to music lovers throughout the country. What do you think these talented musicians wore?

In the ROARING TWENTIES

children wore ...

PETER PAN COLLARS
Children wore 'Peter Pan' collars inspired by the stage costumes of J.M. Barrie's story.

AND

ZIP-UP CLOTHES
At the end of the 1920s, zips started to be used on children's dresses and rompers, making it easier for them to dress themselves.

BUT NOT ...

LONG TROUSERS
Instead of trousers, boys under 12 years old wore shorts with knee-high socks all year round.

Gone went the undergarments of petticoats and stays, which had made girls' clothing so restrictive, and in came looser, lighter washable clothing. Instead of wearing short dresses, little boys were put into a new outfit called a romper suit, which allowed for rough and tumble play. Colour became gendered; blue became linked with boys and pink with girls.

factory workers wore ...

FLAT CAPS
Men wore flat caps or shop caps, which are similar to today's baseball caps.

AND

HOUSE APRONS
Female workers wore 'house aprons', which were like baggy dresses, topped with an additional apron that tied at the waist.

BUT NOT ...

HOOPED SKIRTS
Big, hooped skirts that had previously been fashionable were banned as factory workers had to operate dangerous machinery.

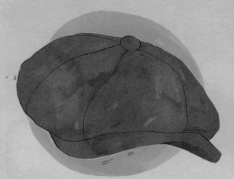  

The new factories offered better paying jobs for most working men and women but they were loud, dirty and dangerous. Men wore sturdy shoes and coveralls to protect them from the grime and machinery. Under their aprons, working women wore dresses made out of rayon, a popular artificial silk that was cheaper and easier to clean than real silk.

flappers wore ...

BARE ARMS AND LEGS
Showing your arms and legs was seen as radical, as before then women kept their limbs covered.

AND

SHORT, LOOSE DRESSES
Underneath their loose dresses, women wore corset-like 'flatteners' to compress their busts and have a more boyish shape.

BUT NOT ...

LONG, FLOWING HAIR
Long hair was out, short hair was in! It became so popular the hairstyle was given a name: an 'Eton crop', or as we still call it now, a 'bob'.

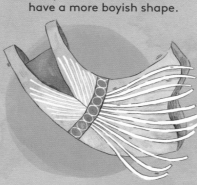

Flappers loved fashion designers Coco Chanel and Elsa Schiaparelli for their sensationally low-cut, drop-waisted short dresses. They shimmied and sparkled in their beaded dresses as they danced. Their shockingly short hair was often adorned with feathered headbands or covered with bell-shaped cloche hats pulled down to just above the eyes.

jazz musicians wore ...

COLLAR PINS
Collars were detachable so collar pins and clips were essential accessories to keep them in place.

AND

FLASHY FOOTWEAR
New shoe styles emerged including the two-toned wing-tip spectator shoes and white shoe covers called 'spats'.

BUT NOT ...

KEYBOARD NECKTIES
Jazz may have been popular but the only keys that pianists played were on the piano. This novelty necktie wasn't invented until the 1980s.

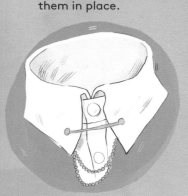

Inspired by the music scene, the jazz suit emerged. Worn by men, it had a very slim-fitting, high-waisted jacket with flared trousers, designed to create an hourglass shape. Breaking away from the past, men's clothes became colourful and more relaxed with stiff, starched collars replaced by shorter, softer collars.

What did people wear in
INDEPENDENT GHANA?

Ghana, 1957

The Republic of Ghana stretches from sandy beaches to rainforests and the open savannah. It is home to leopards and elephants, and contains a wealth of goods from gold to cocoa. These riches have been the source of its trading power as well as its exploitation by the British, Dutch and Portuguese. In 1957, Ghana became the first sub-Saharan African country to gain its independence from colonial rule. Under its first prime minister Dr Kwame Nkrumah, the country was inspired to demand change. Ghana's empowerment was reflected in people's clothing styles, particularly that of Nkrumah, who wore traditional *kente* cloth when he became prime minister, to mark the country's independence from Britain.

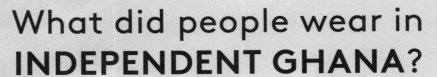

BOWLER HATS

SUNGLASSES

WRAPPER

WOOLLY MITTENS

CHELSEA BOOTS

KABA AND SLIT

Journalists

Newspapers like the *Evening News* were an important way for Ghanaians to discover information about campaigns, protests and plans to dislodge British rule through its articles, editorials and illustrations. What would journalists have worn when researching for their articles?

Photographers

Celebrated photographers like Felicia Abban captured a liberated Ghana. When not in the studio, they photographed news stories across the city. There were many exciting events and people visiting, including Martin Luther King Jr, Maya Angelou and Queen Elizabeth II! What did Felicia Abban wear to cover some of these events?

WHITE SHIRTS

KENTE CLOTH

SNEAKERS

BACKPACKS

GOLD JEWELLERY

SYMBOLIC FABRIC

Architects

The prime minister wanted Ghana's independence to be reflected in its buildings. Ghanaian architects established a brand-new building style that would later be called Tropical Modernism. They would go on to create cutting-edge designs with modern materials suited for the hot climate. How might architects have dressed?

Artists

Artist and former teacher Theodosia Okoh won the government competition to design a new flag to celebrate Ghana's independence. Red represents the bloodshed in the fight for independence; yellow is for the country's gold; and green is for the land. The black star symbolizes Ghana's liberation. What might artists have chosen to wear?

In INDEPENDENT GHANA

journalists wore ...

SUNGLASSES
Advances in plastic meant that sunglasses could become bolder, chunkier and more colourful.

AND

CHELSEA BOOTS
Bands like The Beatles wore these ankle boots with elasticated panels, making them popular across the world.

BUT NOT ...

BOWLER HATS
Although popular in Britain and in Bolivia in the early 1900s, people here would be more likely to wear a trilby or a traditional Dagomba cap.

As a young adult in a newly liberated country, journalists were exposed to the latest news and fashion trends through their work. They sought to be as stylish as the people they were interviewing, boasting the latest looks including flared trousers and big lapelled shirts with bold patterns.

photographers wore ...

KABA AND SLIT
This red, yellow, green and black outfit worn by Abban reflected the colours of the Ghanaian flag – of blood, gold, land and liberation.

AND

WRAPPER
This decorative piece of cloth can be wrapped around the body as a skirt, baby carrier, dress or headscarf.

BUT NOT ...

WOOLLY MITTENS
Ghana is situated near the equator and is very warm so woolly mittens are not needed.

 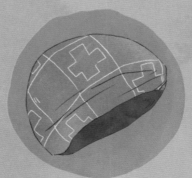 

This iconic outfit from the Ghanaian fashion brand Chez Julie is a modern twist on a traditional classic. It combines kente cloth patterns, but these are printed rather than woven. The printed fabric is used to make a two-piece skirt and ruffled blouse combination called a kaba and slit.

architects wore ...

KENTE CLOTH
Traditionally kente cloth was made on handlooms by men. The cloth's colours have symbolic meanings, and the patterns hold stories.

AND

WHITE SHIRTS
Clothing was often embellished with beautiful embroidery.

BUT NOT ...

SNEAKERS
At this time, sneakers were worn by athletes. They became popular daywear later. People would usually have worn sandals.

Ghanaian architects wore clothes as modern as their buildings, but for big celebrations traditional robes of kente cloth were worn. Kente cloth is woven in narrow strips that are sewn together to make a large cloth that is wrapped around the body and draped over the left shoulder. Kente cloths are treasured heirlooms handed down through families.

artists wore ...

SYMBOLIC FABRIC
Printed on the fabric is a portrait of the first prime minister, Dr Kwame Nkrumah, and the date of Ghana's independence: 6 March 1957.

AND

GOLD JEWELLERY
Gold represented power and spiritual significance in the Kingdom of Asante, and gold continues to be worn for ceremonial occasions.

BUT NOT ...

BACKPACKS
No need for backpacks if you have a wrapper – a piece of cloth that can be wrapped around the body to become a bag or clothing.

Dresses were printed with bold designs on wax-resist or commemorative cloth, which held messages and marked big events. This dress fabric features the country's first prime minister, Dr. Kwame Nkrumah, and messages that celebrate Ghana's independence.

What are we going to WEAR in the FUTURE?

Clothing has many functions. It can protect us from grazes and bumps. It can shield us from the sun and keep us warm against the cold and dry against the damp. It is also a powerful tool that allows us to stand out, blend in or transform. Before the birth of fast fashion, clothing was the costliest thing that most people owned. Now fashion is available everywhere but our planet can't keep up! What are some ways we can enjoy fashion while protecting our planet?

Sustainability

Clothing is one of the greatest polluters, and many garment workers live in poverty. However, there are several fashion designers striving for a better planet. Trailblazing designers are all improving the industry in their own ways: Stella McCartney uses plant-based materials instead of plastics, Bethany Williams makes catwalk clothing from abandoned festival tents, and Sami Miro uses leftover fabric to create stunning new looks.

New from old

Looking back through the years, what could we learn from our ancestors? Could we invest in our clothing like the Elizabethans? Use our clothes to make political statement like the French revolutionaries or weave stories into kente cloth like the Ghanaians? Could you refashion old clothes into new styles? An old dress might become a new T-shirt, old jeans a new bag or perhaps a coat could transform into a waistcoat. How might your clothes make a difference?

Fashion technology

The desire for innovation and exploration has led to the invention of Spandex (a stretchy cloth), safety pins and the disposable nappy. Cleverly engineered clothing has enabled humans to hurtle through space, stop a bullet piercing fabric or plunge into the depths of the sea. As sports technology advances, we will likely see more clothing in our everyday wear inspired by athletes' wardrobes. Look for brands that use recycled plastics to give waste products a new life.

Designers of the future

Over the years there have been many designers who have changed the face of fashion. Mary Quant raised eyebrows, and hemlines, with her miniskirt. Tommy Hilfiger made fashion more accessible with his Adaptive clothing range, which was designed with, and for, people with disabilities, and for over fifty years Vivienne Westwood broke all the style rules, mixing punks and pirates with corsets and kilts. Future fashion is now in your hands. You can decide or design what you want to wear!

Discovering FASHION HISTORY around the WORLD

Museums of all shapes and sizes around the world boast spectacular clothing collections that are bursting with fascinating tales. Held between the fibres of each outfit are stories about the people who wore them.

If you were to give an outfit to a museum, what do you think your clothing would tell someone about you?

- The pattern on your top could tell them your interests.
- The clothing labels show where they were made.
- Wrappers in your pockets might tell them your favourite food!

Step inside a museum and discover the secrets of the past!

WOMAN WITH HAT AND FAN
Greece, 300–200 BCE

The Louvre
Paris, France

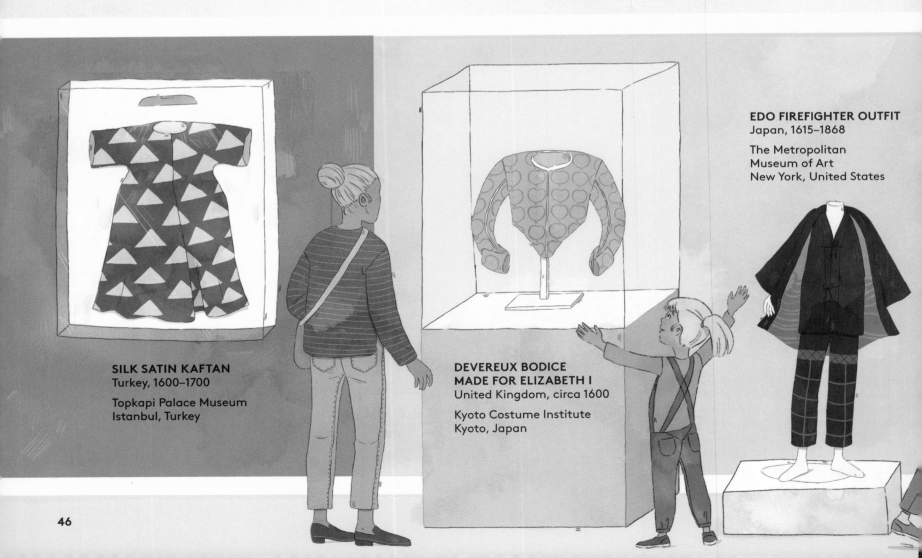

SILK SATIN KAFTAN
Turkey, 1600–1700

Topkapi Palace Museum
Istanbul, Turkey

DEVEREUX BODICE MADE FOR ELIZABETH I
United Kingdom, circa 1600

Kyoto Costume Institute
Kyoto, Japan

EDO FIREFIGHTER OUTFIT
Japan, 1615–1868

The Metropolitan Museum of Art
New York, United States

WOMEN'S CLOTHING FROM AN OLD PEAT-DIGGING HOLE
Denmark, 200 BCE–101 CE

National Museum of Denmark
Copenhagen, Denmark

FEMALE POLO PLAYER
China, 700 CE

Musée Guimet,
Paris, France

ROYAL TAPESTRY TUNIC
Inca state, 1450–1540

Dumbarton Oaks Research
Library and Collection
Washington, D.C.,
United States

SANS-CULOTTE TROUSERS
France, 1789–1799

Los Angeles County
Museum of Art
Los Angeles, United States

DRESS BY COCO CHANEL
France, circa 1925

The Museum at FIT
New York, United States

KABA OUTFIT
Ghana, 1990

V&A Museum
London, United Kingdom

About the author

Katy Canales is the Beatrix Potter Curator. She is responsible for the Beatrix Potter collection of original illustrations, manuscripts and properties that Beatrix Potter left to the National Trust. Katy joined the National Trust after a decade at Young V&A and the V&A Museum. As curator, she produced family-focused exhibitions, displays and public programme events. Katy was the V&A Museum's children's clothing collection specialist. This national collection spans over 400 years and includes everything from Crocs™ to crinolines.

About the illustrator

Erin Vanessa is a former video game producer who's been drawing and painting for most of her life. She runs a lot and loves baking cookies. Erin Vanessa's artwork is a blend of traditional and digital methods. Her inspirations include video games, beautiful food and vintage botanical illustrations. She lives and works in Canada. Erin is the author/illustrator of two picture books: *You Do You-nicorn* and *Swept Away at Witch Camp*.

Phaidon Press Limited
2 Cooperage Yard
London E15 2QR

phaidon.com

First published 2025
© 2025 Phaidon Press Limited
Text © Katy Canales 2025
Illustrations © Erin Vanessa 2025

ISBN 978 1 83866 847 1 (UK edition)
006-0225

A CIP catalogue record for this book is available from the British Library.

Printed in China

Edited by: Alice-May Bermingham
Production by: Rebecca Price
Designed by: Laura Hambleton